MY Amish HERITAGE

Ruth Irene and Ottie Garrett, Jr.

TURNER PUBLISHING COMPANY
PADUCAH, KENTUCKY

Turner®
PUBLISHING COMPANY

412 Broadway • P.O. Box 3101
Paducah, Kentucky 42002-3101
(270) 443-0121

Turner Publishing Company Staff:
Douglas W. Sikes, Publishing Consultant
Shelley R. Davidson, Designer

Library of Congress Control Number:
2003101751
ISBN: 1-56311-869-6

Printed in the United States of America.
Additional copies may be purchased from the publisher.
Limited Edition

Dedication

To my wife, Ruth Irene and to my children, each of you have given me a lifetime of memories.

Contents

Acknowledgements

To Doug Sikes, our publishing consultant, thank you for believing. To Shelley Davidson, our book designer, you can do magic. To Turner Publishing and the entire staff, thank you for believing, and producing such a beautiful book.

To Mark and Katherine Tooley and family, our friendship and ministry is special to us. The song "Crossing Over" is beautiful and your singing is like the voices of angels.

To Pastor James and Raynee Bettermann and Holy Trinity Lutheran Church of Bowling Green, Kentucky. Thank you for your love and God bless you all.

To all our family and friends, we love you all.

~ Ottie and Irene Garrett

Introduction

As a photographer, I have been taking pictures for what seems like all my life. For the past 15 years, I have photographed the Amish people and their lifestyle. For five years during this time, I was partners in a company that produced a series of calendars depicting Amish farms, buggies, horses and quilts. The majority of my calendars were sold to Amish businesses who in turn sold them to the tourists.

There are over 150,000 Old Order Amish in 25 states and because they are not allowed to own or drive cars, they depend on buses, trains, or van drivers to take them to different states to visit family and friends or for business. For years I lived near the Amish and they asked me to take them to weddings, funerals, and sometimes even on family vacations. I had a 15-passenger Ford van and the Amish enjoyed traveling with air conditioning in the summer and heat in the winter, their buggies having neither. During this time I took thousands of pictures of the Amish lifestyle as I transported them and attended their weddings and funerals. I had telephoto and other types of lenses so I could be far away and make the pictures appear quite close. The photos of Amish people I kept for my personal collection and were never published in the calendars. If you look closely at the quilt photos, you can see fingers where the Amish are standing behind the quilts holding them up for the camera. They would never pose for me but as long as I wasn't too obvious with my camera the majority didn't seem to mind at all.

After we were married in 1996, Ruth Irene was fascinated with my photo collection of Amish from different communities. I lived near Kalona, Iowa, so I had a lot of photos of her community, including some of her father, mother, brothers, sister, uncles, cousins, and friends. Because the Amish are not allowed to have cameras or photos, Irene at the age of 22 had none of her childhood or family.

Whenever Irene and I traveled anywhere I would always have my camera at hand. She would help me set up for photo shoots and soon began taking pictures herself. Today we never go anywhere without our camera and Irene takes as many photos as I do.

When the book *Crossing Over* about Ruth Irene's life became a reality, I began sorting all my photos and putting them in order. I had taken pictures of Irene when she was Amish and hundreds after she left as she discovered a new life outside the Amish and met the challenges of a modern society. I soon realized I had captured a progression of moments in time, illustrating a fascinating transition as well as a view into a way foreign to most. Irene had always been beautiful, but this transition was like watching a caterpillar weave its cocoon and emerge as a beautiful butterfly.

This book contains many of my favorite photos of the Amish and of Irene during and after her life as Amish. Each picture is a moment in time, but also a lifetime of memories. I hope you too enjoy this journey.

~ Ottie Garrett Jr.

Chapter 1

Irene

The following pictures are of myself while I was still Amish along with my family and friends and also of my transformation into my new and present life. As I describe a little about the Amish culture, remember that this is the way I grew up and does not necessarily apply to all Amish. All their clothes are homemade and each community has their own Ordnung or set of rules which determines how they dress and what type of buggy they have. A person cannot move to another community without changing their complete wardrobe and buggy. The Ordnung also determines what type of conveniences they are allowed to have, such as running water, indoor plumbing, etc., luxuries forbidden in the more conservative Amish communities.

As a little girl my mother braided my hair and I wore a head covering from the time I was one or two years old. When we went anywhere outside the home, I wore a black bonnet over my head covering until we reached our destination. In cold weather I wore a coat, but always under a shawl pinned around my shoulders. My dresses were made of mostly dark colors with a matching apron, both of them closing with buttons in the back. When we went to church I wore a white starched organdy apron over my dress in place of the usual one and my head covering was black instead of the usual white one. The length of my dresses were about 4 inches above my ankles and I wore black stockings and shoes. When I turned eleven, I no longer wore braids, but put my hair in a bun and could wear the type of dress my mother and sister wore, signifying I was no longer a "little girl." My dress now consisted of three pieces; the dress and a matching cape and apron. The dress now closed in the front and I no longer had buttons, but instead I used straight pins. Only for church did all the unmarried girls and I wear the white starched organdy cape and apron

Winter in early 1996 and it gets cold in Iowa, this day being 30 degrees below zero. When it's really cold we wear a thick scarf under our bonnet, so my head covering is in the pail I'm carrying.

with a black head covering, and our capes crossed in the front. My mother and the rest of the married women always wore a white head covering and their capes pinned straight down the front. Wedding bands, jewelry, or make-up is strictly forbidden.

My father and brothers wore dark, sailor-like trousers with suspenders and lighter colored shirts closing with buttons. They wore black shoes, black felt hats for church and wintertime, and straw hats in the summer. We spoke Pennsylvania Dutch and didn't learn to speak English until we went to school. We had our own one-room schoolhouses and church was not held in church houses but in an appointed Amish home.

Wearing long, dark dresses, black shoes and stockings growing up, I wanted to wear just the opposite when I left the Amish. The first thing I bought was a wrist watch,

white tennis shoes and ankle-length socks, and pastel, lacy, pretty dresses. As you will notice in the pictures, I wore my Amish head covering for awhile, then a Mennonite head covering, and eventually I retired them to my closet and let my hair down and free. Although my Amish clothes are not vital to my salvation as I once believed, I've kept them in remembrance of my past and heritage.

Above: While in Virginia, my cousins and I cross a swinging bridge near our uncle's farm.

At left: My cousins and I are visiting our uncle in Virginia and are headed to their garden to work.

My mother, Martha, my sister, Bertha, and I displaying a quilt that Ottie designed and hired us to make, as a birthday gift to his father in 1995.

On a trip to The Smokey Mountains in Gatlinburg, Tennessee with my sister Bertha, brother Aaron, and seven cousins. I'm the sixth from the left.

I love playing softball and here I'm an outfielder. My glove is a Pro Wilson glove, my favorite.

A cold winter day in Kalona, Iowa and I'm helping out at an Amish farm auction.

Ottie took this picture in 1995 at his home while I'm folding clothes. Because I'm still Amish, I can't bring myself to look at the camera.

Early morning in Kalona, Iowa and I'm driving a two-wheeled cart on my way to teach school.

My cousin, her husband and daughter, my sister and I are on a trip to Florida in May 1996 and we're getting ready to ride an airboat in the Everglades.

For contrast, Ottie took this picture as an English woman was running by me while I'm picking up shells at Lido Key, Florida.

Above: Standing with my cousins, brother, and sister on a mountain top in Virginia. I'm the 5th from the left.

At right: My older brother Benedict and I looking at beautiful Niagara Falls on the Canadian side.

My sister and I collecting shells at Lido Beach, Florida.

On the sidelines of a softball game with young folks at a school in Bloomfield, Iowa where my sister taught.

Family has gathered at a local cemetery in Kalona, Iowa following the funeral of my grandfather.

Above: Wearing my Amish clothes, I'm walking down the aisle to get married at The Bridal Path Wedding Chapel near the Grand Ole Opry.

Top right: Ottie's family held a wedding reception at my father-in-law's house in Glasgow, Ky. and we're getting ready to cut the cake. I had never seen such a beautiful wedding cake. Amish allow wedding cakes but never fancy like this one.

At right: Ottie and I are unwrapping our gifts and I'm holding my first electric sewing machine. Sewing made easy!

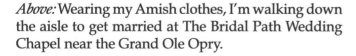

Here I'm standing next to an Osage Orange Tree planted in 1805 at an old fort in Harrodsburg, Kentucky.

Posing with Ottie's two youngest children, Matthew and Samantha after putting flowers on Ottie's mother's grave at The Riverside Cemetery in Attica, In. Putting flowers on a grave was new to me but I thought it was a loving gesture.

Our first home, a two-bedroom house we rented from Freda Jewel near Uno, Kentucky about 15 miles north of Glasgow.

Ottie and I at his dad's house.

Ottie took this photo as I left the courthouse in Munfordville, Kentucky after getting my driver's permit and a photo I.D.

Inset: Ottie Garrett Sr., my father-in-law, giving me instructions on how to operate his 4-wheeler.

Taking Ottie Sr.'s 4-wheeler for a ride around the Haywood subdivision near Glasgow where he and his wife live.

At a restaurant in Iowa, we met Mike Mullane, an astronaut who had been in space six or seven times. He gave us his autograph and posed with Faye and I.

My sister-in-law, Faye, is showing me how to assemble a pretty lamp that she gave me for my 23rd birthday.

This picture was taken at a pretty farm in Alabama.

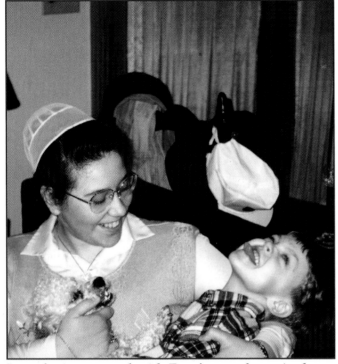

Just playing around with Faye's grandson, Anthony and Ottie Sr.'s dog, Fayzee.

Above: Whenever Ottie gets close to Attica, Indiana, he stops at the Riverside Cemetery to visit the graves of his mother Ersie, her husband Dick Wilson, and Ottie's son Phillip.

Left: On a trip back to Kalona, Iowa, to see my parents, I stopped at Shady Lane School where I used to teach.

Dressed in my robe and ready to sing in the church choir, something I enjoy.

Above: Going over last minute details with our choir director, Jody Wheeler. Notice the Mennonite head covering that I'm wearing. It is smaller in size and I wore this one for awhile after retiring my Amish head covering.

Right: Posing with our Pastor, James A. Bettermann at Holy Trinity Lutheran Church in Bowling Green, Kentucky.

Inside our home in Horse Cave, Kentucky that we rented from Betty and Don Gumm for almost five years and became close friends. The make-up artist, preparing me for a photo session, is from L.A., the photographer on the right, is from New York and her assistant, (not pictured) is from SanFrancisco. They were sent by Glamour Magazine when they did a story about my life as Amish.

With my hair styled and make-up done, I'm ready for the photographer to take the photos for Glamour Magazine.

Above: Ottie and I attending a church picnic in the summer of 1998.

Right: Christmas in 1997 at the Ottie Garrett Sr. home. Ottie and I with his two sons, Monte to my left and Matthew behind me.

Visiting the graves of my brother Tobias and sister Miriam, during one of my return visits to Kalona, Iowa.

Next to me in front of the school where I used to teach, is one of my dearest friends, Starlot Pierce from Greensburg, Kentucky. She and her husband James, (not pictured) traveled with Ottie and I to Kalona, Iowa.

Two of my favorite people, Jake and Edna Schmucker from Goshen, In. Edna is my aunt, (my mother's sister) and they were the first to come visit Ottie and I in Kentucky.

Here I'm being filmed for a special in France. ARTE Television sent their U.S. correspondent, Layla Demay and a cameraman to our home in Horse Cave to film an interview.

In March 2001 while visiting my family in Kalona, I met my sister Bertha in town by coincidence and spent a little time together.

Above: A poster advertising a book signing event at a Barnes and Noble Bookstore.

Right: This was one of my book signings for "Crossing Over" in Reading, Pa. where more than 175 people were present. The book sold out 30 minutes before the signing.

This is Dr. Stephen Glinsky at the Slippery Rock University in Pa. Dr. Glinsky and his wife Ann invited me to speak at the Student Center. Stephen is fluent in German and Ann grew up in Germany, so it was interesting comparing languages.

Arlinda Kessler invited me to speak and do a book signing at Lindsey Wilson College.

An Amish woman stopped to look at "Crossing Over" during a book signing at a Waldenbook Store in New Philadelphia, Ohio.

Ottie's niece Angel and family. From left: Chris, Skyler, and Angel.

Having read "Crossing Over," two former Amish girls came to visit me during a book signing in Greensburg, Kentucky.

A display of Amish clothes for men, women, and children along with Amish paintings in the Greenwood Mall for a book signing.

A graduation ceremony at Barren County High School when I received my G.E.D. from the Superintendent of schools.

My kitchen in our new home and I am getting ready to cut the cake during a house warming. Notice my dishwasher, a convenience I never had before.

Opening gifts on my birthday 2002.

Ottie's nephew Alex and family. From left: Angie, Ashley, Anthony, and Alex.

Ottie's son Monte's new Harley Davidson after he took me for a ride.

Our special guests in our new home. Aunt Edna and Uncle Jake to my left and my cousin Darla, her husband Loren, and daughter Lacey to my right.

Monte and I taking a ride in an amusement park next to Mammoth Cave National Park near our home in Horse Cave, Kentucky.

I still love horses.

Left: During a three-day trial lesson of karate classes in Glasgow, Kentucky. My complete uniform hangs in my closet.

Below: A poppy field near Nashville, Tennessee makes a colorful photo with my maltese, Fluffy.

Dinner at a Japanese Restaurant where they cook in front of you was quite an experience. From right: Brother-in-law, Ben Garrett and wife Sharon, Father-in-law, Ottie Garrett Sr. and wife Pat, Sister-in-law, Faye, and myself.

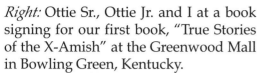

Right: Ottie Sr., Ottie Jr. and I at a book signing for our first book, "True Stories of the X-Amish" at the Greenwood Mall in Bowling Green, Kentucky.

Below: I'm at the Greenwood Mall in Bowling Green doing a presentation and book signing for "Crossing Over."

Seeing my book "Crossing Over" in a bookstore for the first time, at Barnes and Noble in Bowling Green, Kentucky.

Mark and Katherine Tooley and daughters, Sarah Elizabeth and Laura Katherine. Mark and Katherine travel with us to my booksignings to sing Christian songs and the song "Crossing Over" that they wrote and recorded as the theme song.

While on a book signing tour we visited many different places. I'm in front of Independence Hall in Philadelphia, Pennsylvania.

Above: Ottie and I at Niagara Falls. A reflection in the van door shows Ottie's sister Faye taking our picture.

Left: Beautiful Niagara Falls on the U.S. side and I'm using a video camera to film it.

Standing with me from R to L: Faye Talbott, Lewis Sims, State Representative Dottie Sims, Rick Farrant, co-author of "Crossing Over," daughter Amber Farrant, Susie Farrant, and Betty Gumm. Ottie asked Dottie to present Rick and me an Honorable Kentucky Colonels Certificate signed by the Governor of Kentucky.

Posing with Chris Michaels, a professional wrestler and his son Skyler. His real name is Chris Cline and is the husband of Ottie's niece, Angel.

When Ottie and I signed with Polson Productions for a T.V. movie, Beth Polson assigned two Mennonites from Goshen, Indiana to write the screenplay. Don Yost is to my right and Joel Kauffman to my left.

Nanette Varian, Senior Editor for Glamour Magazine came to our home in Horse Cave to write my story. We're having dinner at one of my favorite places, Olive Garden.

Top left: Winter in January 1996 in Kalona, Iowa. My mother and another Amish woman at a farm sale.

Bottom left: My father, Alvin at my Amish home in Kalona, Iowa.

Above: My Amish dress on display for a book signing.

Ottie and I

While on a visit to Kalona, Iowa my former neighbor stops to chat with my sister and me.

This is my grandfather Tobias, 2nd from the left and my grandmother Ruth is 2nd from the right. They are traveling with others to Lancaster, Pennsylvania.

Ottie in his favorite van in the Smokey Mountains.

This is one the publicity photos that Ottie took in his "studio."

I'm parasailing while on vacation in Florida. This is not for the faint in heart and to make matters worse, I can't swim. I enjoyed it and Ottie was petrified.

Ottie and I on the General Jackson for an evening dinner cruise on the Cumberland River in Nashville, Tennessee.

Chapter 2

Scenery

The following photos are of scenery in the Amish country during the changing seasons. They don't have phones or electricity so you won't see any electrical power lines but windmills instead. The windmills are used to pump drinking water from the well to supply tanks for use in the house and barn. The houses have gutters to catch rain water that's channeled into a cistern to use for laundry and other purposes other than drinking.

*Below:*Kalona, Iowa.

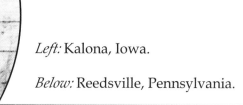

Left: Kalona, Iowa.

Below: Reedsville, Pennsylvania.

Right: Spartansburg, Pennsylvania.

Below: Mount Eaton, Ohio.

Big Valley near Belleville, Pennsylvania.

My cousins and me in Virginia. I'm the second from the left.

Horse Cave, Kentucky.

Grabill, Indiana.

Left: Bloomfield, Iowa.

Below: Kalona, Iowa.

Above: Kidron, Ohio.

Right: Near Munfordville, Kentucky.

Above: Holmes County, Ohio.

Right: Glasgow, Kentucky.

Above; Kalona, Iowa.

Right: South Sunday School building in Kalona, Iowa.

Autumn in Kalona, Iowa. This view is from our family farm looking south toward town. *Inset:* The same scene in the winter. Our farm sets on a hill and all the neighbor children came to our hill for some great sledding.

Left: Wash day at this farm near Kalona, Iowa.

Below: Wheatland, Missouri.

Left: My Amish home north of Kalona, Iowa.

Below: The view of my family's farm looking east from Highway 1, north of Kalona.

The cemetery where my brother, sister, and grandfather are buried.

Opposite page: Kalona, Iowa.

Right: Munfordville, Kentucky.

Below: Holmes County, Ohio.

Big Valley near Belleville, Pennsylvania.

Above: A barn burning near Kalona, Iowa for the movie, "Harvest of Fire," filmed for Hallmark in 1995, starring Patty Duke.

Right: Arthur, Illinois.

Top left: White Gate, Virginia.

Top right: Holmes County, Ohio.

Left: Cashton, Wisconsin.

Right: Lancaster, Pennsylvania.

Below: Near Pinecraft, Florida.

The Kalona Water Tower.

Below: My Amish home in Kalona, Iowa.

Chapter 3

Buggies

All the Amish communities have their own style of buggy. Some have gray, yellow, brown, and white buggies but the majority of Amish have black buggies even though each community has their own style. My community had black buggies made with a particular style, but we had different types. For example, we had open buggies, pick-up buggies, surreys, single buggies that seat two to three people, and two-wheeled carts.

When young men reach twenty one years of age or get married they're given a horse and buggy by their parents. While "English" boys compete dressing up their trucks or cars, Amish boys do the same with their buggies and try to drive the liveliest, prettiest horse. The young men in my community were allowed to use crushed velvet for the seats and the ceiling of the buggy in the color of their choice. They bought their horses from the race track that were disqualified for whatever reason and were quite fast. Racing was not uncommon on Sunday evenings after the young folk singing.

A courting buggy in Grabill, Indiana. This community doesn't allow tops for their buggies.

An old-fashioned sleigh comes in handy for the winters in Kalona Iowa.

Above: Notice the lights on this old-fashioned buggy from Delaware.

Right: A buggy being built in Lancaster, Pennsylvania.

A two-seated gray buggy of Lancaster, Pennsylvania.

This buggy is used for tourists in Lancaster, Pennsylvania.

Notice the white buggies in the barn, only used by the Nebraska Amish. Belleville, Pennsylvania.

These shiny, pretty, yellow buggies with black bottoms are found in the Big Valley near Belleville, Pennsylvania.

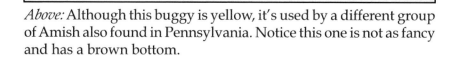

Above: Although this buggy is yellow, it's used by a different group of Amish also found in Pennsylvania. Notice this one is not as fancy and has a brown bottom.

Right: The brown buggies are found in Lawrence County near New Wilmington, Pennsylvania.

A cute miniature rig for this couple in Shipshewana, Indiana.

Amish buggy shops make fancy carriages for the "English" to use in cities where carriage rides are available.

A rainy day in Kentucky.

This type of buggy found only in Medford, Wisconsin. The smoke stack coming out of the buggy is connected to a wood burning stove. In the spring the stove is removed and the wheels put back on.

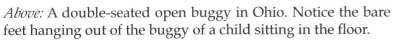

Above: A double-seated open buggy in Ohio. Notice the bare feet hanging out of the buggy of a child sitting in the floor.

Right: Shopping day for this family in Holmes County. Ohio.

Notice the cart being pulled behind the two-wheeled cart in Ohio. In some communities, women don't wear the black bonnet over the white head covering when going somewhere.

Above: Two buggies from Kalona, Iowa. An open, single-seated, pick-up buggy on the left and my uncle is in the single-seated, open buggy on the right.

Right: A two-seated, pick-up buggy in Elkhart County, Indiana. Room for the family and supplies.

Above: Everyone dressed in Sunday best, going home from church near Horse Cave, Kentucky.

Right: Men always sit in the front and women in the back. Women only drive when the men are not along. Logston Valley, Kentucky.

Amish near Glasgow, Kentucky.

An Amish home in Kalona, Iowa. Most Amish like to plant a lot of flowers. The elderly man on the porch used this buggy for courting when he was young. It's been restored by his son-in-law and still used today.

This buggy belongs to a young single man near Shipshewana, Indiana. Look closely for the radio antenna on the top of his buggy.

A two-wheeled cart with fenders near Arthur, Illinois.

This photo was taken near Kalona, Iowa. This man is saving time by hooking a power-take-off unit, wagon, and manure spreader to a two wheeled cart.

A lot of reflector tape on this buggy near Yoder, Kansas.

Notice the blinker on the top of this buggy near Ludington, Michigan.

Above: These are typical buggies used in Kalona, Iowa.

Right: A pick-up buggy with side racks in Ohio.

Below: An Amish funeral procession headed for the cemetery in Illinois.

Left: Three brothers, who are my cousins are headed to town, Kalona, Iowa.

Below: A young man's courting buggy next to the family's flower garden in Daviess County, near Montgomery, Indiana. Notice the reflector tape and other decorations on the buggy and the horse's harness.

Some Amish take pride in their horses and like them to be lively. Lancaster, Pennsylvania.

Below: This style of buggy is unique found in Grabill, Indiana. Children ride in the back out of the weather and the parents up front.

This type of buggy is mainly used for funerals to carry the coffin to the cemetery. Holmes County. Ohio.

A new pick-up buggy.

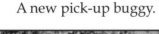

This is a bench wagon, matching the buggies found in the Big Valley in Pennsylvania. Each district in every community has one to transport the foldable, backless, wooden church benches to the home where church is being held.

Flea market and auction in Ohio.

Above: These family buggies are located in Chouteau, Oklahoma.

Right: This buggy was seen in Kidron, Ohio at the famous Kidron Sale.

Above: Buggies outside an Amish school. Notice the two-wheeled cart with a top on the far end.

Left: This buggy is made of metal and has shelves built into it for hauling home-baked goodies to the Farmers' Market in Ludington, Michigan. Notice the flashing light on top.

New and used buggies for sale at this buggy shop near Winesburg, Ohio.

In this community, tops on buggies are not allowed. Bowling Green, Missouri.

A typical two-seated buggy in Texas.

Left: Buggies and cars don't mix and the buggy always loses. Ludington, Michigan.

Below: Buggies don't get flats, but the wheel sometimes falls off. Wouldn't Triple AAA love this call?

No one was killed or even hurt in this accident near Kalona, Iowa.

Chapter 4

Quilts

The quilts in the following pictures are all homemade. Amish have treadle sewing machines which they use to piece the quilts, but the quilting is all done by hand. You will notice many different designs and the vibrant colors. Most of the Amish make these beautiful quilts to sell to the tourists, but are not allowed to have such bright-colored, fancy ones for their own use.

These pictures were taken on Amish farms and quilt shops where the Amish willingly set up their quilts for the photo shoot to be placed in Ottie's calendars. Each quilt maker may slightly change a design to her liking and give it a name. I don't know all the names, but will do my best to give the name for each one correctly. Take notice how some quilts are appliquéd, embroidered, or pieced. A plain top quilt is one that isn't pieced, but has a design quilted into it. Enjoy the beauty of each one.

Ruby's cube broken star.
Cashton, Wisconsin.

Top left: Country Love. Aylmer Ontario, Canada

Top Right: Sweetheart. Kalona, Iowa.

Right: Country Love. Lancaster, Pennsylvania.

Right: Ocean Wave With Hearts. Bird In Hand, Pennsylvania.

Below left: Wedding Ring. Grabill, Indiana.

Below right: Plain top with decorative border. Aylmer Ontario, Canada

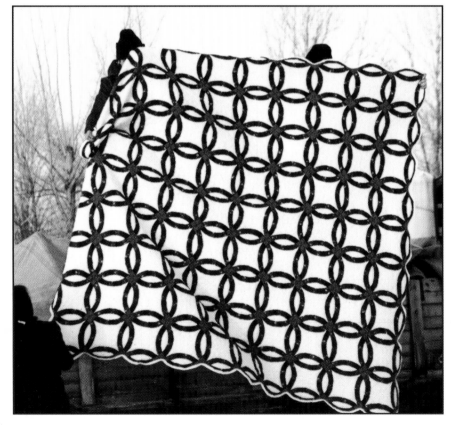

Left: Spring Bouquet. Groffdale, Pennsylvania.

Above: Dahlia. Lancaster, Pennsylvania.

Unknown design from
Daviess County, Indiana.

Nautical Star, the only quilt I know that has a copyright. The price for most quilts are $600 to $1,200 but this one cost $2,400 in 1995. Intercourse, Pennsylvania.

Mariner's Star. Groffdale, Pennsylvania.

Above: Appliquéd Flower. New Holland, Pennsylvania.

Right: Broken Lone Star. Middlefield, Ohio.

Left: Mariner's Compass. Utica, Minnesota.

Below: Preparing a quilt for the photo. Utica, Minnesota.

Bear Claw. Daviess County, Indiana.

Hearts and Flowers. Bear Lake, Pennsylvania.

Above: Star Spin. Middlefield, Ohio.

Right: Chrysalis. Lancaster, Pennsylvania.

Spider Web. Lancaster, Pennsylvania.

Below: Girls getting ready to hold up the quilt for the photo. Conewango Valley, Pennsylvania.

Log Cabin Star Fan. Charm, Ohio.

Left: Spring Bouquet. Groffdale, Pennsylvania.

Below: Country Love. Intercourse, Pennsylvania.

Above: Preparing to hold up the quilt in Aylmer, Ontario, Canada.

Right: Trip Around The World. Cashton, Wisconsin.

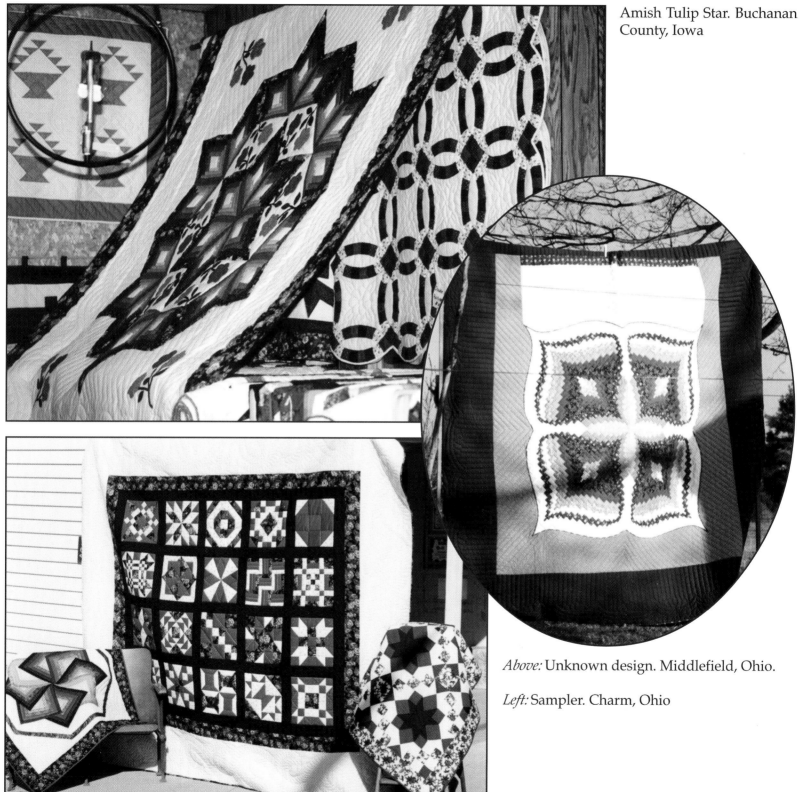

Amish Tulip Star. Buchanan County, Iowa

Above: Unknown design. Middlefield, Ohio.

Left: Sampler. Charm, Ohio

Above left: Two girls from West Union, Ohio holding a Log Cabin Heart.

Above right: Cathedral Star. Strasburg, Pennsylvania.

Right: Unknown design in New Holland, Pennsylvania.

Left: Tulip Appliqué Patchwork. Dover, Deleware.

Bottom left: Broken Star. Shippensburg, Pennsylvania.

Bottom right: Wedding Ring. Lancaster, Pennsylvania.

Chapter 5

Agriculture and Animals

The pictures in this section take you right into the middle of all the work that needs to be done on a farm. Many are filled with so much activity, they look like they could come to life. You will see young boys working in the field, being taught by their father. Women and especially girls are not excluded when haymaking or harvesting needs to be done.

Above: Ohio Farm.

Left: Stephenville, Texas.

Lancaster, Pennsylvania.

Kalona, Iowa. Notice the lugs on the back wheels of this steel-wheeled tractor. Rubber tires are not permitted on tractors, preventing them from being used on the road like a car.

Huntsville, Tennessee.

Farming lessons in Ohio.

Center: In Park City, Kentucky, Swartzentruber Amish women hired by an "English" neighbor plant tobacco. These Amish grow and use tobacco themselves.

Left: Glasgow, Kentucky.

Lucas, Kentucky.

Bird In Hand, Pennsylvania.

Daviess County, Indiana.

Dover, Deleware.

Daviess County, Indiana.

Clark, Missouri.

Clark, Missouri. Notice the old-fashioned push mower. Power mowers are not allowed in this community. My community had power mowers but didn't allow riding mowers.

Above: Rebersburg, Pennsylvania. Notice the mule on the left. Mules are only used by Pennsylvania Amish. Bringing in the hay was sometimes my job during hay making.

Right: Grabill, Indiana.

Above: Kalona, Iowa. Loading oat shocks for thrashing. One thrashing machine is shared by several families and all those using it help each other until everyone's oats are thrashed. Our job on this day was to feed 12 to 15 men who were very hungry.

Right: Holmes County, Ohio.

Right: Ethridge, Tennessee.

Below: Holmes County, Ohio.

Training mules for "English" in Misssouri.

Berlin, Ohio.

Huntington, Tennessee.

Horse Cave, Kentucky.

Lucas, Kentucky.

Top left: Holmes County, Ohio.

Top right: Hillsboro, Wisconsin.

Left: Bowling Green, Missouri.

Holmes County, Ohio.

Above: Winesburg, Ohio.

Right: Shipshewana, Indiana.

Top left: Iowa.

Top right and bottom: Ohio.

Kalona, Iowa. Wash Day at my Amish home.

Vernon, Kentucky.

Aylmer Ontario, Canada. This treadmill is the power that runs the washing machine inside, instead of a gas engine.

Buchanan County, Iowa.

Top left: Llamas in Alabama.

Top right: Pets in Wisconsin.

Right: West Union, Ohio.

"Eat Mor Chikun."

Above: "Where's Mom? I'm hungry."

Left: Feeding time.

"I hate heights."

Brahma bull in Texas.

Beaver in Iowa.

"Come on in, I dare you."

Left: "Y'all move over."

Bottom left: Coyote in Iowa.

Bottom right: Lost.

"Can you smell me now?"

"Come on, we gotta go."

Right: Hog heaven.

"Where's Pete?"

"Mom, wait for me!"

"What!"

"I bet you can't see me."

"I need a haircut."

Right: "Hello."

"Don't take my picture, I'm an Amish dog!"

"Ouch, wow that's hot!"

"Bye Bye."

Chapter 6

Schools

Amish have their own parochial one-room schoolhouses and do not go to public schools. Education beyond the eighth grade is not permitted, believing that knowledge in farming and homemaking is much more important for their young people. Their future is already determined and seeking education for "careers of the world" is not acceptable.

School for me started at 9:00 after helping milk the cows by hand, helping with the last minute breakfast preparations, and trying to get the dishes done before my brothers and I walked the quarter mile to school. School began with a roll call, a Bible story, singing two songs, and reciting the weekly Bible verse and a prayer, most often the Lord's Prayer done in English or German. Although we spoke Pennsylvania Dutch at home, English was used at school and all our studies were in English. This enabled us to become fluent in English,

Kalona, Iowa.

in order to communicate with the outside world. Our studies were Arithmetic, Social Studies, Reading, Vocabulary, English, Spelling, Writing, Health, and a small amount of Science and Art. I excelled in my favorite subjects, English and Spelling, winning a fair share of spelling bees.

For lunch our mother packed the old-fashioned lunch buckets with home-made sandwiches, a container of canned fruit, and cake or cookies. Sometimes we had goodies like cherry cobbler or apple crisp, usually leftovers from supper the night before. In the wintertime, she would sometimes pack egg or cheese sandwiches and soup that we laid on the kerosene stove to get warm by lunch time. For dessert we had a container of homemade ice cream that we had buried in the snow outside to keep it frozen. We didn't spend a lot of time eating lunch because the noon recess was forty-five minutes, the longest one of the day and fifteen minutes for the other two recesses.

For fifteen minutes after the noon recess of very physically active games, the teacher read from select story books. Punishment in school for minor offences was standing with your nose in the corner or a circle drawn on the blackboard. Other times we had to sweep the classroom during recess or similar duties after school. However, if a child gets a spanking in school he/she will most likely get one at home too. When school was over for the day, we promptly went home to do chores that needed to be done before it was time to milk the cows.

All Amish teachers have no more than an eighth grade education and can begin teaching at 17 years old. My sister teaches school today and I taught one year before leaving the Amish. I had fifteen students and taught all eight grades.

Above and left:
Kalona, Iowa.

Drakesville, Iowa.

Otterville, Iowa.

Buchanan County, Iowa.

Mt Eaton, Ohio.

Chouteau, Oklahoma.

Right: Mio, Michigan.

Below: Ludington, Michigan.

Left and below: Glasgow, Kentucky.

Above: Bowling Green, Missouri.

Right: Mansfield, Missouri.

Left and below: Lancaster, Pennsylvania.

Chapter 7

Children

This section contains photos of children and teenagers. The majority of the Amish are Old Order even though each community is not alike. There are stricter groups known as Swartzentruber, Nebraska, Reno, Byler, and the list goes on. Unless the caption under each picture specifies what type of Amish, they are Old Order Amish. These pictures were taken from many different Amish communities so you may notice the variation of dress styles.

Amish have an average of eight children per family. They are farmers and since everything is done manually, having a large family is important. It is also against their Ordnung to use any form of birth control. The oldest children in the family tend to have more responsibilities at a much younger age than their younger siblings. Even so, all the children have work and responsibility at an early age. Amish firmly believe in corporal punishment.

My chores began at three to four years of age, like helping my older brothers gather eggs from the henhouse, bringing in firewood for the wood burning stove, setting the table, and helping with the dishes. As I got older, my duties increased like baking bread, cooking, helping my mother with whatever needed to be done or helping the men folk with certain chores. My oldest brother however, started doing work far beyond his age. At six years old he was driving a team of Percheron horses with a wagon load of corn into town to have it ground, besides doing many other chores that were equally dangerous. If the oldest children in an Amish family are girls they have the same responsibilities as boys would have.

Someone once prompted me with this question, "Was it hard growing up Amish?" I replied, "No, because I grew up not knowing any other way."

Above: A little girl doing the mowing. The majority of Amish children go barefoot in the summertime.

Left: A girl in Kentucky laying out uncut noodles to dry.

Below: A young boy eating a noodle as they dry in the sun.

An auction outside Munfordville, Kentucky. Amish love auctions where they exchange community news.

Left: A little girl curiously looks at an "English" man as she follows her mother.

Below: Young girls at work, possibly fetching a jug of kerosene.

Recess at a school in Holmes Co., Ohio.

Below: A brother and sister on their way to school in Glasgow, Kentucky.

Left: More children on their way to school.

Left: Someone asking this young girl for directions or she's being offered a ride.

Boys at play in Park City, Kentucky. They are Swartzentruber Amish, the strictest of the Old Order Amish.

A family returning home, Red Cross, Kentucky.

Top left: A young boy at work disking a field in Clark, Missouri.

Top right: Riding a horse is a mode of transportation for this girl in West Union, Ohio.

Left: Young boys help their mother by bringing in the laundry from the clothesline. Etheridge, Tennessee.

Dressed in Sunday clothes, three boys at play after church.

Above: A long walk home from school.

A softball game at school during recess.

Young Swartzentruber Amish girls near Mount Eaton, Ohio.

This young girl playing with a pet raccoon.

These girls are visiting in Lancaster, Pennsylvania and they're aware their picture is being taken.

Top left: Two girls near Mount Eaton, Ohio. They appear to be delivering a note with a message.

Top right: Getting the mail like these boys are, is something that's anticipated every day. Because they don't have phones, Amish mostly rely on the postal service for news from family and friends living in other states.

Right: Children in Ohio going home from school.

Left: Amish children are shy and hide from "English" strangers until their parents meet them. This little boy is doing so as Ottie pulled in .

Below: These boys from Lancaster, Pennsylvania are pretending their pretzel rods are cigars. My community did not allow the use of tobacco but some communities grow and use it.

Swartzentruber Amish children playing with their wagon near Park City, Kentucky. Notice the style of the little boy's haircut, used only in certain communities but not in the community where I grew up.

Two brothers at Wal-Mart in Glasgow, Kentucky.

The beginning of a new school year for these children in Glasgow, Kentucky.

A young man from Buchanan County, Iowa feeding sea gulls in Texas on the Gulf of Mexico.

More young people from Buchanan County, Iowa feeding sea gulls.

A group of young men near Munfordville, Kentucky, discussing whatever young men discuss.

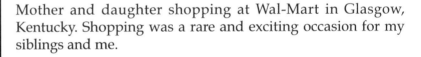

Mother and daughter shopping at Wal-Mart in Glasgow, Kentucky. Shopping was a rare and exciting occasion for my siblings and me.

Above: Gathering the family's mail near Berlin, Ohio.

Right: Playtime on the family's trampoline for these girls near Farmerstown, Ohio.

Opposite page: Notice the faceless doll this little Swartzentruber Amish girl is playing with near Mt. Hope, Ohio.

Right: Where bicycles are allowed for transportation, women ride them too. Picture taken near Mt. Hope, Ohio.

Below: Boys near Mt Eaton, Ohio riding their bicycles, a mode of transportation allowed only in some communities.

Children near Georgetown, Pennsylvania on roller blades, another mode of transportation allowed in some communities.

Father and sons near Shipshewana, Indiana.

Little boys near Mt. Hope, Ohio are trying to hide from the camera while waiting in the buggy for their parents.

Swartzentruber Amish girls near Apple Creek, Ohio are mesmerized by the camera.

Amish near Horse Cave, Kentucky are headed home.

Above: A family near Lancaster, Pennsylvania, where the gray buggies are dominant.

Right: Swartzentruber Amish boys, quite young, are driving home. Amish children begin driving the family's trusted horse at an early age.

Swartzentruber Amish from Park City, Kentucky shopping at Wal-Mart in Glasgow.

This family is not Amish, but belong to a group of Plain People in Indiana. Notice the license plate, something buggies are required to have in Indiana.

Little boys riding on the back of a pick-up buggy near Lancaster, Pennsylvania. One of them is trying to hide his face from the camera, something all children are taught to do.

Children waiting in the family's buggy near Vernon, Kentucky.

Chapter 8

Farms

You will notice that the farms in the following pictures are definitely not alike. Some look very fine and well-kept while others quite the opposite. While most Old Order Amish take pride in their farm's appearance, Swartzentruber and similar strict groups would think that to be vain and are discouraged from planting very many flowers.

Amish farms are very large due to the fact they milk cows for an income and need a lot of horses to do the field work. It also takes a lot of space to store the crops they raise to feed the livestock. Having large families is important in order to take care of a farm this size, therefore needing large houses and gardens to provide enough food and shelter.

White Gate, Virginia.

Left: Lucas, Kentucky.

Below: LaGrange, Indiana.

Kalona, Iowa.

Spartansburg, Pennsylvania.

LaGrange, Indiana.

Cashton, Wisconsin

Left: A Mennonite farmer in Kalona, Iowa.

Below: Intercourse, Pennsylvania.

Right: Belleville, Pennsylvania.

Below: Aylmer Ontario, Canada.

Kalona, Iowa

Right: Shipshewana, Indiana.

Below: Kalona, Iowa.

Atlanta, Missouri.

Above: White Gate, Virginia.

Right: Nappanee, Indiana.

Guthrie, Kentucky. Amish here are quite liberal. They use rubber tire tractors as cars for their transportation during the week and the horse and buggy on Sunday.

Below: Clark, Missouri.

Holmes County, Ohio.

Shippensburg, Pennsylvania.

Holmes County, Ohio.

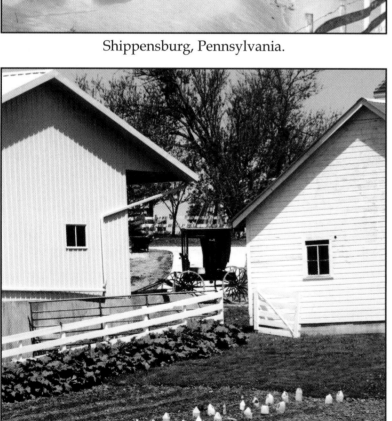

Kalona, Iowa.

Cashton, Wisconsin.

Above: Kalona, Iowa

Sugarcreek, Ohio.

LaGrange, Indiana.

Holmes County, Ohio.

Kalona, Iowa. Some like displaying their wealth.

Belleville, Pennsylvania.

Chapter 9

Adults

This section mostly contains photos of adults and unless each caption specifies what kind of Amish they are, they are Old Order Amish. I will also point out the men who are bishops. Bishops are the leaders and hold the highest position in the Amish. Each community is divided into districts and each district usually has one bishop, two to three ministers, and a deacon. Only a bishop is allowed to perform ceremonies such as baptisms, funerals, and weddings. The ministers conduct the church services and the deacon will read scripture passages but never do any preaching. The deacon will also pay members a visit when they break a rule in the Ordnung. Amish women are subservient to men and are never heard in church. When church members vote on issues, women are allowed to vote, but the final decision lies with the bishop and ministers.

Although we speak Pennsylvania Dutch in every day life, the church services are conducted in the High German. The songs are sung in a slow, drawn-out manner from the German Lieder Sammelung or Ausbund. The scriptures are read from a German Bible (King James Version) and the prayers from a German prayer book called the Christenpflicht. We sat on narrow, backless, wooden benches and the church services are usually three hours long. Each family in each district takes turns to have church at their home and feeds the whole congregation afterwards. The meal consists of huge stacks of homemade bread, jam or jelly and always the Amish peanut butter spread along with pickled red beets, pickles, tea and coffee.

Above: Mennonites in Pinecraft, Florida.

Left: The two men talking are Swartzentruber Amish and the man behind them is Old Order. Holmes County, Ohio.

Below: Waiting to cross the road in Holmes County, Ohio.

Telephones are not allowed in their homes but it's an important tool and hard to do without. Photo taken in Dunnville, Kentucky.

Swartzentruber Amish shopping in Glasgow, Kentucky.

Pushing the cart is one of the bishops of Glasgow, Kentucky. He and his wife are shopping at Wal-Mart.

Making a trip to town for shopping is a rare event so they make it worthwhile. These Amish are Swartzentruber near Park City, Kentucky.

Deep pockets. Claire, Michigan.

Swartzentruber Amish at a flea market near Claire, Michigan.

These Swartzentruber Amish are traveling in a converted school bus. They are not allowed to hire a driver for traveling but may use commercial transportation like buses or trains. No Amish are allowed to fly.

An Amish farm auction near Munfordville, Kentucky. The women are Swartzentruber Amish.

Father shows his daughter photo note cards at the family's store in Pennsylvania.

Fetching a horse for work near Vernon, Kentucky.

Right: These women can't believe what they're seeing. They're from Buchanan County, Iowa visiting Niagara Falls in New York.

Below: Fall weather along Lake Michigan. These women are from Iowa.

Driving in traffic.

Above: Proud of his work, Daniel L. Miller, an Amish artist near Munfordville, Kentucky. Notice the telephone in his shop window. Some Old Order Amish groups allow a phone in the barn or outbuilding.

Right: Foggy morning on an Amish farm near Vernon, Kentucky.

Amish gather for an auction in Logsdon Valley near Munfordville, Kentucky.

Amish in Pinecraft, Florida. Hundreds of Amish from different communities go live in Florida for the cold winter months. Here they rent or own homes that have telephones, electricity, and air conditioning. Bicycles are used for transportation instead of the horse and buggy.

A battery powered scooter/wheelchair helps this elderly man get around in Mt. Hope, Ohio.

Women helping in the family's furniture shop. Notice the woman on the left is wearing a head scarf, something women wear when working in the garden or yard.

Attending an auction even on crutches. Notice that the woman's cape is pinned straight down the middle which means she's married.

A cold day to be traveling in Hillsboro, Wisconsin.

The man and the two women in the front are Swartzentruber Amish and the rest in the picture are Old Order.

Notice the difference in these women's clothes. The two women with dark clothes and black bonnets are Swartzentruber Amish. The two walking by them are Old Order but a bit liberal and they are from Munfordville, Kentucky.

The women with the white head coverings are married.

Swartzentruber Amish men on business in Glasgow, Kentucky.

After a church service in Missouri. Notice the white aprons and the black head coverings the little girls are wearing, only worn for church.

Amish bishops and ministers from many different communities gather here for the National Steering Committee Meeting to discuss matters most important to all Amish. This meeting is being held in the Big Valley near Belleville, Pennsylvania.

Left: Amish always kneel for the two prayers during the church service. Church is sometimes held in the barn like this one in Annabel, Missouri.

Below: Church services usually last three hours or more.

Chapter 10

Miscellaneous

For the conclusion, this section contains a variety of unique road signs found in the Amish country, along with a few other interesting ones. I hope these photos have given you a visual insight into the Amish world as you cross the bridge of time.

Covered bridge in West Union, Ohio and a Michigan road sign.

On a trip.

Michigan

Kentucky

Above: Checking out the horses at the race track.

Right: Amish saw mill.

Liberty, Kentucky.

Delaware.

Windsor, Missouri. A grocery store owned and operated by Amish.

An Amish style restaurant in Ohio.

Iowa.

Most stores in rural Amish areas provide a hitching rail. *Top right:* An example of a hitching post.

Without phones, mail is important.

Phones are always needed.

This is the type wash machine used by most Amish, powered by a gas engine.

Above: A buggy shop in Winesburg, Ohio.

Right: An Amish carpenter business hires a driver to take them to their job sites.

*Above:*Van drivers for the Amish line up and wait for their passengers at a National Steering Committee Meeting in Lancaster, Pennsylvania.

Left: An unusual vehicle for travel. Notice the woman in the window.

Above: Auction in Indiana.

Left: Ready for auction.

Top left: Iowa.

Top right: Minnesota.

Below: Selling produce in Glasgow, Kentucky.

One of the paintings done by Robert Howell from some of Ottie's photographs.

Above: Amish painter D.L. Miller in Munfordville, Kentucky, copying Ottie's photograph. This artist used more than a dozen of Ottie's photos to do a series of paintings.

Right: D.L. Miller's finished painting.

Young boys racing their horses near Horse Cave, Kentucky.